New Vanguard · 86

OSPREY
PUBLISHING

M109 155mm Self-Propelled Howitzer 1960–2005

Steven J Zaloga · Illustrated by Tony Bryan

First published in 2005 by Osprey Publishing, Midland House,
West Way, Botley, Oxford OX2 0PH, UK
443 Park Avenue South, New York, NY 10016, USA
Email: info@ospreypublishing.com

A CIP catalog record for this book is available from the British Library.

ISBN 1 84176 631 3

Editor: Katherine Venn
Design: Melissa Orrom Swan
Index by Alison Worthington
Originated by Grasmere Digital Imaging, Leeds, UK
Printed in China through World Print Ltd.

05 06 07 08 09   10 9 8 7 6 5 4 3 2 1

For a catalog of all books published by Osprey please contact:

NORTH AMERICA
Osprey Direct, 2427 Bond Street, University Park, IL 60466, USA
E-mail: info@ospreydirectusa.com

ALL OTHER REGIONS
Osprey Direct UK, P.O. Box 140, Wellingborough,
Northants, NN8 2FA, UK
E-mail: info@ospreydirect.co.uk

www.ospreypublishing.com

Author's note

The author is indebted for the help of many people who assisted on this
project, and would like to thank Lee Ness, Christopher Foss, Pierre Touzin,
Rob Gronovius, John Charvat, Leif Hellstrom, Simon Dunstan, and Just Probst.
Thanks also to Randy Hackenburg and Jay Graybeal of the Military History
Institute at the Army War College in Carlisle Barracks, PA; Charles Lemons
and Candace Fuller of the Patton Museum at Ft Knox, Kentucky, and Dr. Jack
Atwater and Alan Killinger of the US Army Ordnance Museum at Aberdeen
Proving Ground for their help with access to their superb archives.

Artist's note

The author may care to note that prints of the original paintings from which
the color plates in this book were prepared are available for private sale. All
reproduction copyright whatsoever is retained by the Publishers. All inquiries
should be addressed to:

tonybill@tiscali.co.uk

The Publishers regret that they can enter into no correspondence upon this
matter.

M109 155MM SELF-PROPELLED HOWITZER 1960–2005

INTRODUCTION

The M109 155mm self-propelled howitzer pioneered the configuration of modern mechanized artillery. During the 1960s it became the standard artillery weapon for NATO's mechanized forces, and was built in greater numbers than any post-1945 self-propelled howitzer outside the Soviet Union. The M109 has seen combat in many regions, including use in the Vietnam War, in the Arab–Israeli conflicts, the Iran–Iraq war, and the Gulf wars of 1990–91 and 2003. Although the US Army started programs to replace it in the 1980s, these new designs failed for a variety of reasons, leaving the dependable M109 in service. In recent years there have been many programs to modernize the M109, which will extend its service life for a decade or more into the future.

COLD WAR ORIGINS

In the late 1940s the US Army attempted to replace the mechanized artillery designs of World War II with a new generation of vehicles. There were two objectives in these programs: to adopt novel features, such as a

The M109 155mm self-propelled howitzer was the most influential artillery design of the post-World War II period. This is an M109A2 of the 1-3d Artillery, 2d Armored Division at Hood, Texas in 1983. (Author)

3

rotating turret for the cannon, as well as acquiring a common chassis to simplify logistics. In World War II the standard US Army mechanized artillery vehicle was the M7 105mm howitzer motor carriage (HMC), which was supplemented in 1945 by a small number of M37 105mm HMCs. After the war, US armored division commanders concluded that there was a need for at least one battalion of 155mm howitzers to supplement the 105mm howitzers. A small number of M41 155mm HMCs were built in 1945 before demobilization put a quick end to armored vehicle production. There was an immediate need for new vehicles once the Cold War heated up in the late 1940s, because both the M37 105mm HMC and M41 155mm HMC programs were so few in numbers. Both the M37 and M41 were based on the M24 light tank chassis, and so their successors, the M52 105mm Howitzer Self-Propelled (HSP) and the M44 155mm HSP, were based on the M24 replacement, the M41 light tank. While this facilitated a rapid development of the new artillery vehicles, it had its disadvantages. Developers hoped to move away from the open casemate configuration of previous self-propelled guns to adopt a fully enclosed turret which would protect the crew, as well as offering a greater traverse. While this proved practical with the M52 105mm HSP, the chassis was too small to accommodate the recoil forces of the larger 155mm howitzer, so the archaic open casemate configuration was retained. When both vehicles were adopted for service in the early 1950s, it was immediately clear that the designs were flawed. After its rushed development the M52 105mm HSP was plagued with technical problems, and the configuration of the M44 155mm HSP was deficient. As a result, the US Army began to study replacements in 1952, even before the new types had fully entered service.

From a tactical standpoint, the Army wanted a fully protected turret such as that pioneered on the M52 105mm HSP. Since the advent of the first generation of artillery location radars in the 1950s, artillery had become more vulnerable to counter-battery fire from enemy artillery. Location radars could track the ballistic path of incoming artillery projectiles back to their point of origin, thereby making accurate counter-battery fire possible for the first time. In addition, the practice of simply

One of the T195E1 pilots is seen here at Aberdeen Proving Ground in 1961. There are several differences between the pilots and the production M108 including the configuration of the headlights, the stowage bin on the turret front, and the side skirts. (MHI)

mating existing towed artillery to tank chassis was abandoned in favor of developing artillery specifically designed for vehicle mounting. The new vehicle also needed a wide chassis with a large turret ring diameter, better to absorb the strong recoil forces of large-caliber howitzers.

The Ordnance Tank-Automotive Command (OTAC) authorized development of the T195 110mm HSP and the related 156mm T196 in April 1953, and wooden mock-ups were built. Artillery officers soon asked what advantage would be gained by adopting odd calibers such as 110mm and 156mm, and these were abandoned in 1956 in favor of the existing 105mm and 155mm calibers. The Army was also interested in developing a self-propelled howitzer that could cross inland waterways without special kits, and so these configurations were explored as well. With its far-flung commitments around the globe, the Army wanted the vehicles to be as light as possible, and innovations in aluminum fabrication suggested that aluminum armor would be one way to accomplish this objective. Once the design studies were reviewed, a meeting was held at the Detroit Tank Arsenal in October 1956 to begin the engineering development phase of the program. The T196 155mm HSP proved to be the more complicated design as it incorporated a power traverse for the weapon and additional recoil spades at the rear of the vehicle to absorb the heavier recoil forces of the larger howitzer. As a result, the T196 pilot arrived six months later than the T195, being completed in March 1959. The T195 went into trials first, and during tests at Ft Knox the pilot suffered from serious suspension and final drive problems.

While the testing program was going on, the Army was debating the future of armored vehicle propulsion. Although the Army had relied on gasoline engines for a half-century, new diesel engines offered better fuel economy, especially in the case of heavy vehicles such as tanks, so from 1959 diesel engines were gradually introduced into all of its tracked combat vehicles. Since the new self-propelled howitzer program was in hiatus until the power-train problems could be ironed out, OTAC

ne of the T196E1 pilots at
erdeen Proving Ground in
62. This shows the second
yle of headlight with a wire
ush-guard, replaced on the
oduction M109 with a full
otective cover. (MHI)

ordered the modification of the T195 and T196 with diesel engines. Two of the four pilots were reconfigured with diesel engines, and their designations were changed to T195E1 and T196E1 HSP. Tests on the modified vehicles resumed in 1960, but once again, serious problems with the suspension and final drives forced OTAC to suspend the tests and halt planned production of the new vehicles. Greater attention was paid to production engineering, and two new construction pilots of each type were manufactured. The new vehicles were subjected to trials in 1961, culminating in a 4,000-mile test at Aberdeen Proving Ground (APG). The trials demonstrated that the modifications had worked, and so the Army approved limited production of both the T195E1 and T196E1 in

The M108 105mm SPH served only a few years with the US Army before being withdrawn in favor of the M109. This example with extemporized camouflage, belongs to B/1-40th Artillery at Ft Sill in 1966 shortly before being deployed to Vietnam. (US Army)

The largest user of the M109 aside from the US Army was the German Bundeswehr, which used them from 1966. They were modified to the M109G configuration, which had a new breech better able to withstand maximum propellant charges. This example has a canvas weather cover over the muzzle brake. (Pierre Touzin)

December 1961. Production started in late 1962, and after the new vehicles had been subjected to further trials, the production contract was extended another year. In July 1963, the T195E1 and T196E1 were accepted as standard equipment by the Army and type classified as the M108 105mm HSP and M109 155mm HSP. For the sake of clarity, the M108 and M109 will be referred to by their later and more common designation of self-propelled howitzers (SPH) from this point on, even though the change did not occur until the late 1960s.

Production of the M108 was short-lived, ending in 1963 after about 355 had been built. By this time, the US Army favored the larger 155mm howitzer and decided to standardize this caliber in the armored and mechanized infantry divisions instead of using a mixture of 105mm and 155mm howitzers. This was yet another step in the increase of divisional firepower, from the 75mm gun of World War I, to the 105mm howitzer of World War II, to the 155mm howitzer of the Cold War years. As a result of this change, production of the M109 155mm SPH for US forces was substantially greater than the M108, totaling 2,111 vehicles – 1,961 for the Army and 150 for the Marine Corps. In addition, 1,675 M109s were manufactured for international clients. All of the M108s and M109s were manufactured at the Cleveland Tank Plant, with the facility being managed by Cadillac the first two years, Chrysler for the third year of production, and the Allison Division of General Motors until 1969 when production in Cleveland ended.

The first M109 155mm SPH entered US Army service in June 1963. It was a considerable leap forward in artillery design and quickly attracted the attention of several NATO armies. Germany was in the process of modernizing the Bundeswehr under the *Heeresstruktur* 2 program, and wanted to replace its 124 old M44A1 155mm SPHs with a more modern design. The M109 was selected and was delivered from 1964, eventually totaling 609 vehicles; Germany became the second-largest user of the M109.

The new M109 design was a watershed in artillery development. Although the earlier M52 105mm HSP had pioneered the turreted howitzer concept, its technical shortcomings meant that it did not have a profound influence on howitzer design. The small turret ring was not easily adapted to improved weapons, and the shift from 105mm to 155mm cannon did not bode well for its longevity. In contrast, the M109

used a chassis specifically developed for artillery, rather than a converted tank hull. As a result, it was wide enough to accommodate a large-diameter turret ring, and it was spacious enough inside to incorporate further improvements. The split recoil spades proved much more practical than earlier designs such as the M12 and M40 155mm SPG, which used a full-width spade that interfered with access to the fighting compartment. The engine and transmission were robust and permitted further weight increase on the chassis without adverse effects to automotive performance.

The M109 had ten crew members. Of these, six traveled on the M109 itself, while four crewmen traveled on the accompanying M548 cargo carrier that was used to deliver additional ammunition. Aside from the driver in the forward left section of the hull, the other five crewmen were in the turret/fighting compartment. The gunner was in the left front of the turret near the main gun controls, with the assistant gunner on the opposite side in the forward right side of the turret. Behind them were two cannoneers who assisted the gunners. In the right rear of the turret on the seat below the large hatch was the chief of section (CS). When the M109 was deployed for action, four crewmen remained in the turret, but the chief of section dismounted to direct the other cannoneers who were responsible for the ammunition supply, and the driver often dismounted as well. The 155mm rounds were large and heavy, requiring two men to carry them during sustained fire missions. Other crewmen were needed to prepare the propelling charges, fuze the ammunition and perform associated tasks.

An M109 had a maximum rate of fire of four rounds per minute, which could be sustained for about three minutes. Over longer periods of time, the rate of fire decreased to about one round per minute. The maximum range was nine miles (14.6km) with standard ammunition, and 12 miles (19.3km) with rocket-assisted projectiles. The primary instrument for aiming the weapon was the M117 panoramic telescope located in the left forward corner of the turret and operated by the

An M109 155mm SPH with improvised winter camouflage of Battery C, 2-33d Artillery during the Certain Shield training exercise in Germany on January 22 1973. In subsequent years, all M109s in US Army service were upgraded to the M109A1 configuration. (US Army)

gunner. An M118A1 elbow telescope was mounted on the opposite side of the gun and was used for targets that were visible to the gun crew for direct fire engagements. The turret was power-driven with the controls located on the gunner's side. Access to the turret was ample, in part to allow adequate ventilation during firing to prevent excessive fumes from accumulating inside the turret. There was a large hatch on either side of the turret, two hatches in the roof, a hatch at the rear of the turret, and a large access hatch at the rear of the hull between the two recoil spades.

US M109 PRODUCTION

Year	M109	M109A1B	M109A2	M109A5
1962–69 (US)	2,111			
1962–69 (FMS)	1,675			
1974			99	
1975			222	
1976			169	
1977			183	
1978			178	
1979		71	45	
1980		231	70	
1981		335	53	
1982		276	260	
1983		199	120	
1984		194	27	
1985		231	75	
1986		209		
1987		256		
1988		106		
1989		119		
1990		117		
1991		182		
1992		105		
1993		110		
1994				10
1995–2003				127
Total	**3,786**	**2,741**	**1,501**	**137**

 # FIRST COMBAT: VIETNAM

Although the M109 155mm SPH was designed primarily for high-intensity combat in the NATO/Warsaw Pact confrontation in Central Europe, it was never used in combat in this theater. Instead, the M108 and M109 first saw active service in Vietnam. Given the nature of the terrain and the US Army's growing reliance on air-mobility in Vietnam, there was not a great demand for self-propelled artillery. No armored or mechanized infantry divisions were posted to Vietnam, so there was no self-propelled artillery organic to the divisions stationed there. The Army preferred lighter towed artillery, which could be easily moved by helicopter, or the more powerful, long-range M107 175mm SPG and M110 8in SPH for long-range artillery missions. However, a small number of self-propelled howitzer battalions were eventually deployed to Vietnam, serving with corps-level artillery formations. Self-propelled guns proved useful in Vietnam because of the style of warfare. The US Army established fire support bases throughout South Vietnam to provide artillery coverage for infantry operations. They

were often in the midst of "bandit country," with Vietcong guerillas operating on all sides of the base. Full 360-degree coverage was therefore essential, and towed artillery had a very limited traverse. In contrast, the M108 and M109 SPH could offer full coverage.

Although the M108 was considered obsolete in Europe, the first field artillery battalion sent to Vietnam was the 3-6th Artillery which was equipped with the M108 and was deployed to Pleiku on June 17, 1966. About the same time, the first medium self-propelled field artillery battalion was sent to Southeast Asia, the 2-35th Artillery which deployed near Xuan Loc with the 23d Artillery Group, equipped with the M109. A second M108 battalion followed in October 1966, the 1-40th Artillery, which served with the 108th Artillery Group near Dong Ha. Besides their service in artillery battalions attached at corps level, the M109 155mm SPHs were also deployed in armored cavalry squadrons that had an organic battery of six howitzers. When the 11th Armored Cavalry Regiment deployed to Vietnam in September 1966, it was accompanied by three squadron artillery batteries with a total of 18 M109 155mm SPHs. By 1969 the Army had deployed five M109 and two M108 artillery battalions to Vietnam out of a total of 57 battalions stationed there, or about a tenth of the total. By the middle of 1968 there were 36 M108 and 108 M109 self-propelled howitzers in action in Vietnam, less than a tenth of the Army's inventory.

While many of the assignments of the light and medium self-propelled artillery battalions in Vietnam involved traditional indirect fire missions, the tactics were quite unlike those planned for a European conflict. Self-propelled howitzers were usually deployed in static positions at fire bases, instead of being used in a mobile role as in Europe. The M108 and M109 howitzers were usually parked in defensive emplacements, often configured in a standard fashion with a sandbag or earthen berm in front of the vehicle, and sometimes supplemented by a chain-link fence to catch RPG-2 and RPG-7 rocket grenades. Protected ammunition stowage racks were located behind the vehicle, with sandbagged crew quarters on either

One of the first self-propelled artillery battalions to arrive in Vietnam, the 3-6th Artillery, deployed to Pleiku in June 1966. An M108 of Battery A is seen here at a fire base near Pleiku on June 28 1969. The markings on the left stowage bin identify it as being attached to the I Field Force Vietnam, and the turret is painted with kill markings. (MHI)

side. The configuration of the emplacements varied somewhat depending on the location of the fire base. Many units oriented the berms towards the expected enemy positions, but some units, such as the 23d Artillery Group, configured them with full 360-degree protective coverage because of the threat of attack from all directions.

The configurations of the fire bases varied enormously. In the 23d Artillery Group, for example, fire bases would often consist of a battalion headquarters with one of its own batteries, but with two batteries from other battalions with mixed equipment. So a fire base might have a battery of M109s, along with a battery of 105mm towed howitzers and a mixed 8in M110/175mm M107 self-propelled battery. The batteries of a battalion might be scattered 60km apart from one another at different fire bases. The fire support bases became quite sophisticated. The Fire Support Coordination Center (FSCC) was the communications hub of the base, which received fire requests, coordinated the artillery missions with US and ARVN (Army of the Republic of Vietnam), and assigned the fire missions to the specific battery. The exception was on the occasions when a battery was assigned for direct support of a specific maneuver battalion, in which case, the FSCC was cut from the communications loop to speed up response time. The FSCC also operated an artillery warning control center that coordinated artillery strikes with any US strike aircraft in the area, since it could be hazardous for low-flying strike aircraft or helicopters to operate in an area targeted by the artillery. The FSCC often operated observation towers for close-range missions and base defense, as well as artillery location radars to detect the location of North Vietnamese artillery and rocket units. If the artillery had to support maneuver units that were outside the range of established bases, temporary and less elaborate fire support patrol bases were established, although these were more dangerous for the artillery crews. Fire Base Maury I, for example, was hastily constructed but even before bulldozers

arrived to create the emplacements, the Vietcong staged an attack on the night of May 9, 1968. In the resulting skirmish, five M109s and two M548 ammunition transporters were destroyed, one of the heaviest losses of self-propelled howitzers in a single incident. Under constant threat of attack, batteries were often assigned defensive sectors for direct fire against intruders, and on many bases, .50-caliber machine-gun nests were set up at every howitzer emplacement for additional self-defense.

The US Marine Corps used the M109 155mm SPH in Vietnam as well, though in smaller numbers. The 4-11th Marines and 4-12th Marines both used the M109, and the Marine experiences paralleled those of the Army. The self-propelled howitzers tended to be used from static locations, and the Marines found that towed artillery was often more useful because it was easier to move these guns by helicopter.

"The Flower Pot," an M109 of 2-32d Artillery in a revetment at Fire Support Base Rivera in the Binh Tuy-Ham Tan district while supporting the 199th Light Infantry Brigade on September 8, 1970. The ammunition is stowed in sandbagged shelters behind the M109 for protection. (US Army)

This M109 of Battery B, 2-138th Artillery, was named "Bullwinkle" after the popular TV cartoon moose, and is seen at Fire Support Base Tomahawk south of Phu Bai in September 1969. This battalion was from the Kentucky National Guard, and served in Vietnam for one year from October 1968. The bumper code identifies it as being attached to XXIV Corps Artillery. (US Army)

The Army's self-propelled battalions began to be withdrawn from Vietnam in 1969 as the burden of the fighting was shifted to the South Vietnamese. Both M108 battalions were gone by mid-1970 and the last M109 battalion had left by the end of 1971. The Vietnam War did not have a profound impact on US Army self-propelled artillery development because the numbers deployed were on a very small scale compared to deployments in Europe. The Vietnam experience did increase Army interest in extending the effective range of the 155mm howitzer, however, after frequent encounters with the Soviet M46 130mm gun that was widely used by the North Vietnamese People's Army. The Vietnam War was the one and only time that the M108 105mm SPH saw combat.

LONG-RANGE FIREPOWER

Several factors led the US Army to reconsider the need for further development and production of the M109. The original design requirements for the M109 155mm SPH insisted that the weapon have longer range than the previous M44 155mm SPH. This was accomplished by using a stronger propelling charge. However, once in service it became evident that the blast pressure from this super-charge was excessive, sometimes damaging the vehicle and injuring the crew. Extended range was also sought after the Vietnam experience that highlighted the better range of some Soviet weapons.

An alternate approach to increasing range was the extension of the length of the cannon barrel. In May 1967, the Army began to study a longer-range version of the M109. A longer 155mm cannon, the XM185 howitzer, was already being developed for other applications and this was easily adapted to the M109. It had a barrel length of 39 calibers compared to the 20-caliber tube of the original M126 cannon on the M109.[1] The XM185 cannon was mounted on three pilot vehicles and subjected to field trials at the artillery school at Ft Sill starting in April 1969. The new weapon extended the range from nine miles (14.6km) to 11 miles (18km) using the M118 Zone 8 propelling charge. The results were so satisfactory that the Army decided to modify its M109s with this new weapon, and it was classified as standard in August 1970 as the M109A1 with the M185 155mm cannon. Depot conversions began in 1973 and continued until April 1981 with all US Army M109s being converted. The first unit was equipped with the M109A1 in May 1973. The M109A1 included many changes to the basic M109: besides the new gun tube, a larger hydraulic motor was needed, along with improvements to the equilibrator. Heavier torsion bars were added to the front two road-wheel stations to accommodate the heavier weight, and a new gun lock was added at the front end of the hull instead of on the engine deck. A weapon-

The M109A1 introduced a new, longer gun, which is seen near full elevation in this view. This vehicle is from the Infantry Division during the 77 Reforger exercise near einreid, Germany. It is finished the typical Seventh Army camouflage scheme of the period, and the green encircled triangle indicates that this vehicle was serving with the Opposing Forces during the wargame. (US Army)

---

1 A caliber refers to the bore diameter. So for a 155mm howitzer, a barrel 20 calibers long means a barrel 3,100mm long or about 10ft 1in.

mounted rammer was added to replace the cab-mounted rammer in the M109.

By the early 1970s, there was a growing shortage of M109 SPHS. To begin with, the weapon had proved so satisfactory that the US Army was intent on adopting it as the standard divisional artillery weapon. Other armies, especially those in NATO, were also interested in modernizing their artillery arsenals, and there was no other suitable design available in Europe. Production was restarted both to satisfy US requirements and to fulfill export orders. By 1972, more than 1,500 M109s had been ordered by international customers through the Foreign Military Sales (FMS) and Military Assistance Program (MAP).

As conversion of the M109A1 was underway, the Army began a "Mid-Life Improvement" program, as a number of modifications had been recommended during its first decade of service. The new M178 gun mount was developed to better handle the recoil forces of the more powerful M185 cannon. The new rocket-assisted projectiles that were being developed were longer than the standard rounds, requiring different stowage arrangements. To accommodate these, and to increase on-board ammunition stowage, a bustle was added to the rear of the turret that raised the onboard load from 28 to 36 rounds. An all-weather ballistic cover was fitted over the panoramic sight in place of the previous cover that left an exposed circular opening when the periscopic sight was in use. A counter-balanced travel lock was added on the front. The seldom-used flotation system was removed, along with its redundant inflation system. An improved engine was adopted with better fuel injectors and a more efficient turbo-charger. The Army decided to adopt these changes in two ways. More M109s were needed, so the new configuration was accepted for production in November 1975 as the M109A2. In addition,

This rear view of an M109A2 of Battery C, 1-3d Artillery, 2d Armored Division, Ft Hood, Texas, shows the distinctive change of the M109A2/A3 upgrade: the extended bustle rack in the center of the turret rear that permitted more ammunition to be carried. This photo also shows the recoil spades extended for firing. (Author)

The ballistic cover over the gunner's sight is clearly visible on this M109A2/A3 during the joint US–Egyptian Bright Star exercises in 1982. The M109A2 was the new-construction vehicle, and the -A3 the upgraded model, and they are impossible to distinguish externally. (US Army)

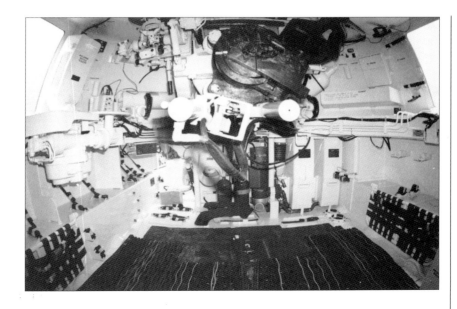

the Army decided to gradually add the Mid-Life Improvement PIP (Product Improvement Program) kit to older M109A1s, and the upgraded vehicles were designated as the M109A3. The new production M109A2 and the converted M109A3 were externally identical.

Production of the M109A2 began at Bowen-McLaughlin-York (BMY) and the Army funded the production of 823 new vehicles in Fiscal Years 1976–85. Instead of being manufactured at the Cleveland Tank Plant, production was started at the BMY plant in York, Pennsylvania, the firm which is most closely associated with the M109. BMY became part of United Defense in the mid-1990s, along with another well-known armored vehicle manufacturer, FMC Corp. that built the M113 APC and M2/M3 Bradley. The M109A2 first entered service with the 24th Infantry Division (Mechanized) at Ft Stewart in early 1980. Conversion of the M109A1 to M109A3 began at Letterkenny Army Depot in October 1979, and was completed in April 1984. There were a number of minor upgrades to the M109A2 and -A3 in service, such as the installation of the AN/PRC-68 radio, starting in January 1983.

In parallel to the manufacture of the M109A2, BMY also restarted M109A1 production for export clients in 1979. The new production vehicles were designated as M109A1B to distinguish them from the previous conversions. They had a number of small internal changes including deletion of the flotation feature, but otherwise the M109A1B did not have the full M109A2 upgrade. A total of 2,741 new M109A1B vehicles were manufactured by BMY from 1979 to 1993 when production finally ended. The M109A1B could also be upgraded to M109A2 standards using the M109A1 Mid-Life PIP kit and the M178 mount kit. These conversions were designated as M109A3B.

ENHANCING LETHALITY

Even though the M109A1 stayed in production for 20 years, it remained a viable weapon. Unlike NATO main battle tanks, which undergo substantial modernization at least once a decade, artillery weapons do not become obsolete so quickly. The reason is that the self-propelled howitzer itself is only a single element in a complex matrix of artillery systems including fire control centers, artillery location radars, communication systems, and ammunition. While the M109 itself did not change very rapidly, there were many innovations in artillery that improved its performance. Ammunition is the clearest example. The standard round for the 155mm howitzer was the M107 high-explosive projectile. Weighing 92.8lb (42kg), it was filled with 14.6lb (6.6kg) of high-explosive. This was improved in the 1970s with the development of HERA (High-Explosive Rocket-Assisted) projectiles. They offered a longer range than the baseline M107 projectile since they contained an additional 7lb (3kg) rocket charge at the base of the projectile which provided a propulsive boost during flight, and extended the range from 11 miles to 19 miles (18–30km). Like the M107, the M549 HERA projectile was filled with high-explosive.

While such rounds were quite effective against exposed infantry and unprotected equipment, they were less effective against well-entrenched infantry or against armored vehicles. In the early 1960s the US Army developed the first generation of ICMs, or Improved Conventional Munitions. These were "cargo" rounds, relatively thin-walled projectiles filled with small submunitions. A fraction of a second before the projectile reached earth, the time fuze detonated a small burster charge that ejected the submunitions from the base of the projectile, scattering them over a wide area. The first of these was the M449 ICM-AP (Anti-Personnel) which contained 60 M43A1 grenades. The ICM-AP had a larger lethal footprint than a conventional HE projectile. When the submunition struck the ground, a small charge detonated and ejected a high-explosive grenade about six feet in the air which exploded and sprayed high-velocity fragments in all directions. The ICM rounds were first used on a limited scale in 1968 in Vietnam, but the dense jungle foliage of the terrain made them impractical.

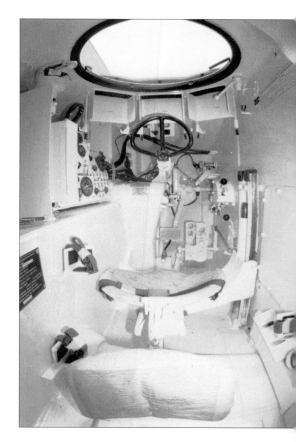

A view of the driver's compartment in a new M109A2. The driver's position was connected to the main fighting compartment in the turret behind, while to the right was the engine. (Author)

The next innovation was the far more important M483 DPICM (Dual-Purpose) round which contained 64 M42 and 32 M46 grenades, small half-pound cylindrical submunitions that were stabilized in flight by a small ribbon that unfurled behind them after separation from the cargo round. The grenades contained a dual-purpose, shaped-charge warhead. On impacting a hard surface, such as the roof of an armored vehicle, the small shaped charge detonated and could penetrate the thin top armor. On hitting the ground, the warhead detonated in the same fashion, and the resulting explosion sent steel fragments in all directions, much like a small grenade. The difference between the two grenades was that the fragmenting shell of the M42 grenade was embossed to create smaller fragments, while the M46 did not have an embossed wall and so shattered into larger fragments. This was followed by the extended-range M864 DPICM projectile that was fitted with a base burner unit at the rear of projectile to expel exhaust gas during flight, reduce drag, and so increase the round's effective range.

The advent of the revolutionary ICM cargo rounds led to interest in other types of novel submunitions, especially mines. Two related types were deployed in the early 1980s, the M692 and M731 ADAM (Area Denial Artillery Munition), and the M718 and M741 RAAM (Remote Anti-Armor Mine). The ADAM projectile contained 36 small, wedge-shaped anti-personnel mines, while the RAAM contained nine larger cylindrical anti-tank mines. The projectile contained a timer that dispersed the mines through the base of the projectile in flight. The mines became armed on contact with the ground, and contained self-destruct timers if they had not detonated in a prescribed time. The advantage of such weapons compared to conventional mines was that they could be deployed behind enemy lines to cut lines of communication or to channel retreating enemy forces. A single M109 could lay 2,400 ADAM mines or 600 RAAM mines in an hour. The standard package was a minefield 400 meters square containing six ADAM and 24 RAAM which could be laid by five salvoes from a standard six-gun battery in about two minutes. These types were accepted for use on the M109 in January 1976: the ADAM entered production in 1976, and the RAAM in 1978.

The most secret of the M109 ammunition types were the "special" projectiles. The US Army first deployed nuclear 155mm ammunition in the mid-1950s. The most common type assigned for delivery by the M109 was the M454 AFAP (Artillery-Fired Atomic Projectile) containing a W48 plutonium fission warhead. With a yield equivalent to about 100 tons of high-explosive, it was first manufactured in 1962 and about 3,000 were deployed. It was to be replaced by the M785 armed with the W82 nuclear device in 1990, but the end of the Cold War prompted the US government to withdraw tactical nuclear artillery warheads from service in the early 1990s.

The stable-mate of the M109A2/A3 was the M548A1 cargo carrier, which was used in artillery battalions to deliver ammunition. Here, an M548A1 is backed up to an M109A2/A3 at the National Training Center in the Mojave Desert in November 1990. (Author)

Another "special" type was the chemical weapons projectile, and a variety were manufactured until 1969 when the US declared a moratorium on chemical weapons production. The M110 projectile contained mustard gas, while the M121A1 contained GB or VX nerve agent. By the late 1970s these weapons were unserviceable and there was substantial evidence that the Soviet Union was continuing to develop and deploy chemical weapons. This led to the development of the M687 binary projectile. To make these projectiles safer to handle, two inert chemicals were stored separately within the projectile. When it was fired, the plate separating the two canisters ruptured and the chemicals were mixed in flight by the spinning action of the projectile, creating the nerve agent GB. The projectile was split open on impact by a point-detonating fuze. The M687 entered production in December 1987, but this type of weapon was eliminated after the US signed an international treaty banning chemical weapons in 1997.

Besides these various forms of lethal ammunition, the M109 has a variety of other projectiles available, including the M110 (white phosphorous) smoke; M116 (screening and signaling) smoke; M825 (screening) smoke; M485 illumination; and M804 practice projectile. Projectiles must be fuzed before firing, and a variety of fuze types are available depending on the ammunition and the type of target. Standard fuze types include point-detonating fuzes, the mechanical time fuzes, mechanical time and super-quick (MTSQ) fuzes, and proximity fuzes. As in the case of most large-caliber artillery, the M109 uses split ammunition with the propelling charge loaded separately from the projectile. These propelling charges are delivered in a tubular metal container and most types come in several separate sections called increments. The crew can select the number of increments to be used depending on the range to the target.

Until the advent of inertial navigation systems, M109 batteries typically deployed together on fire missions as seen here at the Field Artillery Training Center at Ft Sill, Oklahoma, in December 1991. Until 1986, each battery had six M109s, but under the Div-86 organization, battery strength was increased to eight. (Author)

MIDDLE EAST COMBAT

Following the Vietnam War, the next conflict involving the M109 155mm SPH was the 1973 October War between Israel and Egypt. In 1969 the Israeli Defense Force (IDF) ordered an initial batch of 24 M109 155mm SPHs to supplement their ragged inventory of improvised self-propelled howitzers based on old Sherman tank chassis, and these were used during the 1973 war. One of the clearest lessons of the 1973 war for the IDF was the need for additional modern self-propelled artillery. The quick victories in the 1967 war had allowed the IDF to believe that a tank-centered force could succeed on the modern battlefield, a delusion that was shattered by their heavy initial losses in the 1973 war. Egyptian anti-tank squads armed with RPG-7 rockets and Malyutka anti-tank missiles wreaked havoc on Israeli tank units in the first days of the fighting, as the forward tank units did not have sufficient self-propelled artillery to suppress the infantry anti-tank teams. Following the war, the IDF shifted to a more conventional combined arms approach that required extensive modernization of its artillery force. The M109 force was expanded to 60 vehicles, and all were later converted to M109A1s. In addition, the IDF began a major purchase of the M109A1B, eventually totaling a further 369 vehicles.

By the time of the 1982 Lebanon war, the M109 had been extensively deployed in the IDF mechanized units. While the IDF M109s were widely employed for traditional artillery indirect fire-support missions, the IDF also adapted their tactics to exploit the M109's potential in a direct fire role. These tactics were most commonly used during the fighting for Beirut. Some of the surrounding hills outside the city were located too far away for effective tank gunfire, so the self-propelled howitzers were used instead. In addition, self-propelled howitzers were used in urban fighting during specific assaults where reinforced buildings had to be attacked. The huge high-explosive projectiles of the M109 were found to be very effective in reducing strongpoints, and in some cases, causing the complete collapse of buildings. The need to use the M109 in direct fire in the city itself was partly due to the fact that most contemporary tank guns lack a powerful high-explosive fragmentation round, and the normal anti-armor ammunition is not as effective in destroying concrete structures. In addition, tanks had a hard time fighting in narrow streets since they could not elevate their guns sufficiently to engage snipers on upper stories of buildings. This posed no problem with the M109. When used in this role, the M109 was kept to the rear of a combined arms formation, usually with a Merkava tank unit in front to suppress snipers and RPG gunners at street level.

Israel acquired 24 M109 155mm SPHs shortly before the outbreak of the 1973 war, one of which is seen here. The Sinai fighting convinced the IDF of the need to modernize its neglected artillery branch, and over 300 M109A1s were obtained in the 1970s. (GPO)

One of the lessons of the fighting was the need to provide the M109 with more ammunition. The traditional means of supplying trucks such as unarmored M548 cargo carriers or trucks left them vulnerable to sniper fire and RPG ambush. After the war Urdan (Israel's armament manufacturer) developed an armored ammunition trailer, the Artrail, which can carry an additional 44 rounds of ammunition in protected containers.

Among the export clients for the M109 in the 1970s was Iran, who ordered 50 M109 155mm SPHs. These were later upgraded to M109A1 standards, and a further 390 M109A1B SPHs were obtained in the late 1970s prior to the fall of the Shah and the advent of the Islamic Republic. When war broke out between Iran and Iraq in 1980, Iran was one of the largest operators of the M109 outside NATO. A significant number of M109A1 SPHs were captured by Iraqi forces and apparently, small numbers were put into Iraqi service during the war.

PRECISION-GUIDED MUNITIONS

The 1970s saw the first serious efforts to design guided artillery projectiles that could hit pinpointed targets such as tanks. The US Army started the Copperhead program in 1971, aimed at developing a laser-guided 155mm round that could be fired by the M109. To use the Copperhead, a forward deployed observer such as the M981 FIST-V forward artillery observer vehicle, an Aquila drone, or an OH-58D scout helicopter, would "illuminate" the target with a laser designator. After communicating with the artillery that the target was illuminated, the M109 would fire a Copperhead round into the general area of the target. As the M712 Copperhead descended on the target, the seeker in the nose would detect the reflected laser light, and steer the round against the target using small fins on the projectile. Production began in the early 1980s at a unit cost of about $45,000 per round. Although a very intriguing idea, the projectile proved less formidable in actual use. The

need to carefully coordinate the mission between the M109 and the forward observers made the Copperhead awkward to use in combat, and production ended in the mid-1980s. The one and only combat use was in Iraq in Operation *Desert Storm* in 1991 when about 100 rounds were fired with a high rate of success.

Copperhead was followed in 1988 with the M898 SADARM (Sense-And-Destroy-Armor Munition). The SADARM was a cargo round that contained two tubular submunitions. After being released from the projectile, the submunitions deployed a parachute retarder which slowed the submunition and stopped it from spinning. This was followed by a second parachute that uncaged the electronic sensor and began the target search routine by spinning the submunition in a circular pattern. The search routine starts at a height of about 150 meters, with the millimeter wave radar sensor canted about 30 degrees off the vertical. The spiral pattern of the submunition naturally decreases as the SADARM descends, thereby covering a large circular area below it. On sensing a target, the sensor detonates the warhead which collapses a copper warhead liner into an explosively formed kinetic energy penetrator, and this is propelled at the target at speeds in excess of 2,000 meters per second, easily penetrating the top armor of a tank. The Army had great hopes for SADARM, but the end of the Cold War seriously undermined the rationale for the program as the threat of a massed Soviet tank attack suddenly evaporated. Significant technical difficulties were encountered during testing, but the SADARM finally went into production in 1995. The Army prematurely terminated the program due to rising costs after about 1,000 rounds had been manufactured, and the last was delivered in 2002. As mentioned below, they were first used in combat in Iraq in 2003.

After the disappointing results with the first two generations of guided projectiles, in 1998 the Army started development of the M982

Excalibur 155mm Extended-Range Artillery Projectile (ERAP). In contrast to the two previous programs, the Excalibur is not intended for pinpoint precision, but rather uses the signals from the GPS navigation satellites to provide greater accuracy than conventional, unguided artillery. The projectile carries a DPICM payload of submunitions, so pinpoint accuracy is not necessary. The Army hopes to start production of the Excalibur in 2004 if tests prove successful, and it will be deployed with the M109A6 Paladin.

THE MODERNIZATION DILEMMA: NEW OR REBUILD?

By the late 1970s the US Army self-propelled artillery force was based primarily around the M109A2/A3 vehicles. European NATO members were interested in developing a next-generation self-propelled artillery vehicle, and embarked on the SP-70 program. One of the major innovations in this design was the development of an autoloading system for the ammunition that could increase the firepower of the vehicle. The US Army took a somewhat different approach. In 1969 the US Army Human Engineering Laboratory (HEL) at Aberdeen Proving Ground began an annual set of exercises called HELBAT (Human Engineering Laboratory Battalion Artillery Test), an effort to improve the effectiveness of the field artillery battalions. The early trials concluded that more attention should be focused on the infrastructure supporting the M109, not necessarily the weapon itself. The majority of the accuracy problems were attributed to forward observers or the fire direction center, and the need to modernize these elements of the battalion. One of the first steps was the development and deployment of the M981 FIST-V (Fire Support Team Vehicle), an M113 armored personnel carrier fitted with improved navigational devices, laser rangefinders and observation sensors for the forward observer teams. These were first tested in HELBAT 6 in 1976. The HELBAT tests also suggested that placing an autoloader on the M109 would not solve the rate of fire problem, since once the onboard load of ammunition was expended a modified configuration would still need ammunition delivered in the old, laborious manner. HELBAT began to examine an ammunition delivery system (ADS) that later emerged as the M992 FAASV (see below).

HELBAT also helped the Army to define its future artillery needs. The Army began to study M109 replacements in 1979, a convoluted process that has dragged on for nearly 25 years, and which continues at the time of writing. The lack of a replacement to date is in part a testimony to the basic soundness of the M109 design, and its adaptability to improvements. The first Army study program was ESPAWS (Enhanced Self-Propelled Artillery Weapon System), which advocated a substantial upgrade effort, later judged too expensive. A scaled-back effort called DSWS (Division Support Weapon System) followed in the early 1980s. DSWS eventually spawned three options, including modest improvements to the existing M109A2/A3 fleet, known as HELP (Howitzer Extended Life Program); a more extensive upgrade program called HIP (Howitzer Improvement Program); and examination of an entirely new design, which later led to the Crusader program.

The HELP program primarily focused on reliability upgrades and improvements to the M109's NBC (Nuclear, Biological, Chemical) protective system. A prototype of this upgrade, the M109E4, was delivered in 1983. There was very little pressure to adopt these features as the Army gradually became convinced that more extensive upgrades were needed like those suggested in the HIP program. As a result, the Army deferred this upgrade program until 1990, and confined it to vehicles in National Guard and reserve battalions. The upgraded vehicles were designated as M109A4.

The HIP program examined a variety of potential weapon upgrades from 1985. Three new cannon were examined: the new 58 caliber XM282, the lighter 39-cal. XM283 based on the M198 155mm towed howitzer, and an upgraded 39-cal. XM284 based on the M185 howitzer already used on the M109A2. Several test-bed vehicles, including the M109A3E2 and -E3 were constructed and subjected to trials. The weapon selected for the M109 HIP was the M284 cannon and M182A1 gun mount. Extended range was no longer the Army's main concern, since the divisional artillery was beginning to receive the new MLRS

The M109A5 is upgraded with the gun and mount of the M109A6, but lacks the new turret or its many internal improvements. As a result, it is very difficult to distinguish from the M109A2 and M109A3 vehicles on which it is based. An example from 1-78th Artillery is seen here with an M992 FAASV at Ft Sill. (Author)

(Multiple Launch Rocket System) which was assigned the long-range and counter-battery mission. More important considerations were an improved ability to "shoot-and-scoot". Until the HIP program, US Army self-propelled guns had to be deployed in a static location, their positions carefully surveyed, and the entire battery of guns connected to the fire direction center. As a result the battery was slow to deploy and vulnerable to counter-battery fire from enemy artillery. The new MLRS vehicle had a built-in land navigation system linked to an automated digital fire control system that revolutionized artillery tactics. Individual MLRS launcher vehicles could scoot around the battlefield, deploy quickly to the safest and most convenient location, and open fire within moments of receiving a fire order. After firing, the vehicle could then move off to another location, avoiding enemy counter-battery fire. M109 battalions had such a capability with their jeep-mounted PADS (Position Azimuth Determining System), but the Army now wanted each M109 to have this feature, which was becoming smaller and more economical with the advent of new technologies. The Modular Azimuth Positioning System (MAPS) was developed for the M109 HIP, which used a compact and economical ring-laser gyro for its inertial navigation. The MAPS was linked to a digital ballistic computer and weapon servo control. When a fire order was inputted into the computer, it combined it with location data from the MAPS, and then automatically laid the gun precisely on target. Target data arrived through a new digital communications processor that received orders over a secure radio.

In February 1990, the Army type-classified the HIP as the M109A6, and it was nicknamed "Paladin" after the popular Western novel and TV series about a fast-shooting cowboy gun-slinger. Rather than try to incorporate all these devices in the existing turret, the M109A6 received a new turret, easily distinguishable by its larger size, squared front, and the higher step at the rear of the turret. Low-rate production of the new M109A6 began in September 1991, and the first unit equipped was the 2-17th Field Artillery at Ft Sill in June 1993. The next units equipped were the battalions of the 24th Infantry Division (Mechanized) at Ft Stewart in 1994. The M109A6 was type-classified as standard in April 1996. The original plan was to procure 164 new-production M109A6s, and convert a further 660 older M109A2/A3s. In the end, the US Congress added funding for more vehicles, so a total of 957 were converted by 2003. Remaining M109A2/A3s in National Guard units were converted to the M109A5 configuration

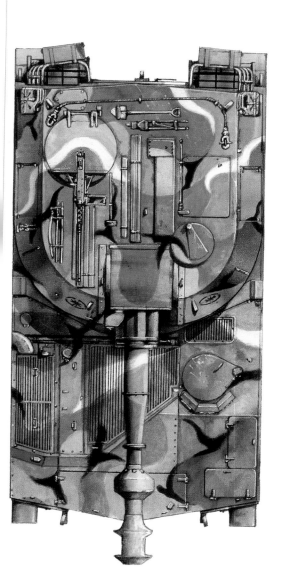

A: M109 155mm SPH, Battery A, 1-14th
Field Artillery, 2d Armored Division,
Ft Hood, Texas, 1976

A

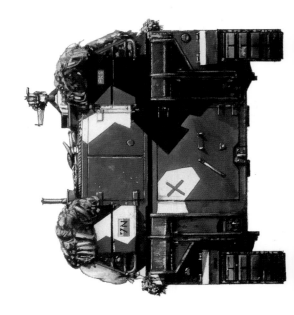

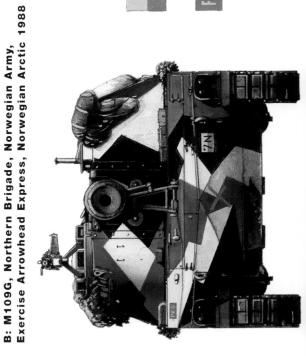

**B: M109G, Northern Brigade, Norwegian Army,
Exercise Arrowhead Express, Norwegian Arctic 1988**

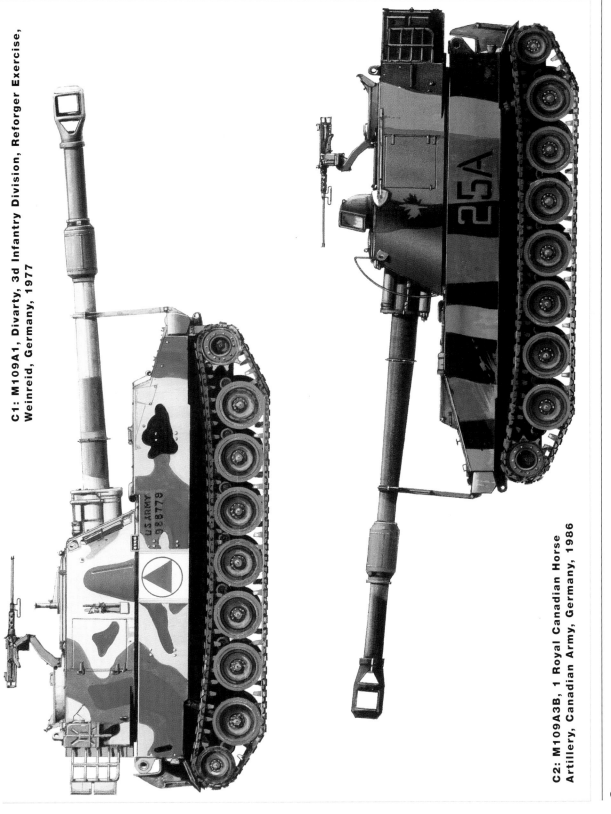

C1: M109A1, Divarty, 3d Infantry Division, Reforger Exercise, Weinreid, Germany, 1977

C2: M109A3B, 1 Royal Canadian Horse Artillery, Canadian Army, Germany, 1986

D: M109A2, FIELD ARTILLERY TRAINING CENTER, FT SILL, OKLAHOMA, 1995

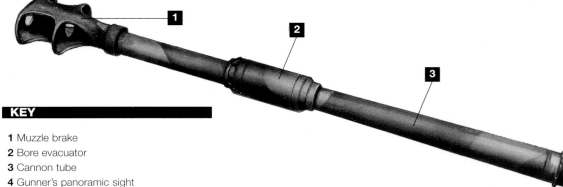

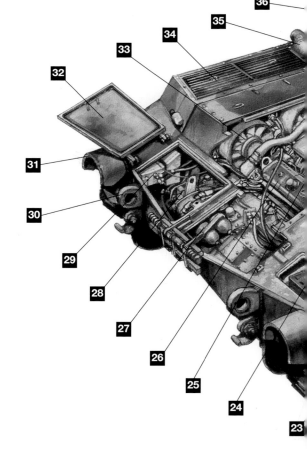

KEY

1 Muzzle brake
2 Bore evacuator
3 Cannon tube
4 Gunner's panoramic sight
5 Gun trunnion
6 Turret lifting ring
7 Ballistic cover for gunner's sight
8 .50-cal. heavy machine gun
9 Commander's cupola
10 Commander's seat
11 Turret bustle
12 Rear turret stowage bin (left side)
13 Projectile stowage
14 Propellant stowage
15 Gun breech
16 Gun rammer assembly
17 Fire extinguisher
18 Manual turret traverse mechanism
19 Driver's seat
20 Driver's instruments
21 Driver's controls
22 Roadwheel
23 Drive sprocket
24 Batteries
25 Diesel engine
26 Engine crankcase
27 Oil filters
28 Transmission
29 Final drive
30 Hull lift hook
31 Armored headlight cover
32 Transmission access panel
33 Engine fans
34 Radiator grill
35 Engine exhaust
36 Recuperator cover

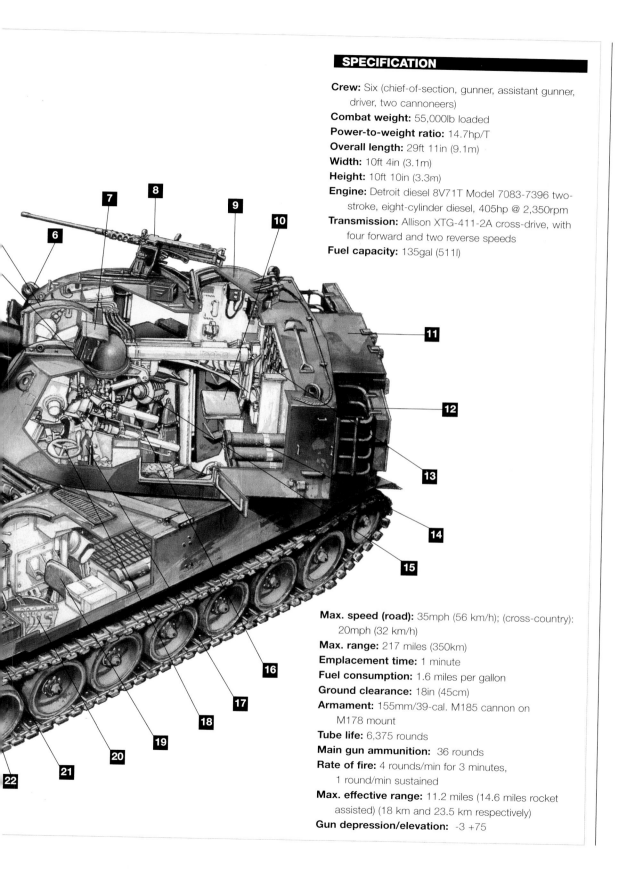

SPECIFICATION

Crew: Six (chief-of-section, gunner, assistant gunner, driver, two cannoneers)

Combat weight: 55,000lb loaded

Power-to-weight ratio: 14.7hp/T

Overall length: 29ft 11in (9.1m)

Width: 10ft 4in (3.1m)

Height: 10ft 10in (3.3m)

Engine: Detroit diesel 8V71T Model 7083-7396 two-stroke, eight-cylinder diesel, 405hp @ 2,350rpm

Transmission: Allison XTG-411-2A cross-drive, with four forward and two reverse speeds

Fuel capacity: 135gal (511l)

Max. speed (road): 35mph (56 km/h); (cross-country): 20mph (32 km/h)

Max. range: 217 miles (350km)

Emplacement time: 1 minute

Fuel consumption: 1.6 miles per gallon

Ground clearance: 18in (45cm)

Armament: 155mm/39-cal. M185 cannon on M178 mount

Tube life: 6,375 rounds

Main gun ammunition: 36 rounds

Rate of fire: 4 rounds/min for 3 minutes, 1 round/min sustained

Max. effective range: 11.2 miles (14.6 miles rocket assisted) (18 km and 23.5 km respectively)

Gun depression/elevation: -3 +75

E: M109A3G, 3./Panzerartilleriebataillon 25, Braunschweig, Germany, 1991

E

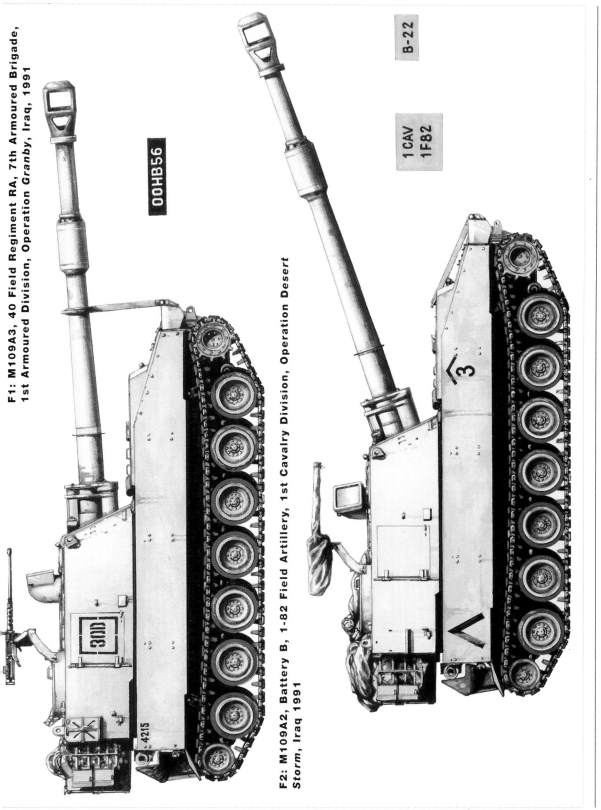

F1: M109A3, 40 Field Regiment RA, 7th Armoured Brigade, 1st Armoured Division, Operation *Granby*, Iraq, 1991

F2: M109A2, Battery B, 1-82 Field Artillery, 1st Cavalry Division, Operation Desert *Storm*, Iraq 1991

F

G: M109A6 Paladin, Battery B, 1-10th Field Artillery, 3d Brigade, 3d Infantry Division (Mechanized), Operation *Iraqi Freedom*, March 2003

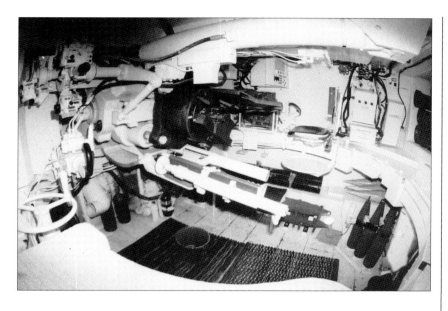

An interior view of the M109A6 Paladin turret. The digital data display for the section commander is evident in the upper center of the picture beyond the gun breech. (Author)

The US Army had planned to replace the M109 with the new M2001 Crusader starting around 2005, but the program was cancelled in 2003. This is a computer illustration of the proposed configuration of the Crusader. (United Defense)

starting in 1995 which used the same gun and mount as the M109A6, but without the extensive turret and fire control upgrades. The M109A5 closely resembles the M109A2/A3 externally and most of the changes are internal.

While the M109A6 program proved to be relatively straightforward, the same was not the case with the design of a new replacement. The Army originally hoped to leap forward by adopting a liquid propellant gun. Such a weapon would have an advantage over conventional powder-based artillery in that the propellant could be gradually sprayed into the combustion area of the gun breech, permitting a carefully regulated detonation that would impart maximum energy on the projectile, while at the same time minimizing the recoil forces on the gun. In the end, this concept proved to be beyond the state-of-the-art and had to be abandoned. By the time that the Army restarted the program in the early 1990s, the Cold War had ended, and other NATO armies were already on the verge of deploying a new generation of 155mm self-propelled guns, such as the British AS-90 Braveheart and the German Panzerhaubitze 2000.

The US Army program emerged in the late 1990s as the XM2001 Crusader 155mm self-propelled gun and the XM2002 armored resupply vehicle. In early 2000 the Department of Defense ordered a major redesign of the Crusader, reducing the armor protection and ammunition stowage in favor of lower weight, so its size shrank from 64 ton to 38 ton. This pushed back initial production until 2005 or later. Finally, in 2002, the Secretary of Defense canceled the program, arguing that the Army needed to shift to lighter vehicles that were easier to deploy. As a result, the self-propelled howitzer requirement was rolled into the Army's Future Combat System program, which means that an M109 replacement will not appear until 2010 or later. Improvements are therefore being planned for the Paladin that will extend the life of this venerable system towards a half-century of service. One direction may be a new longer 52-cal. cannon, which is already being offered to export clients under the name "International Howitzer."

FEEDING THE GUNS

Although the US Army had examined a variety of autoloading systems to speed the rate of fire of its self-propelled artillery, it quickly became clear that the factor most responsible for limiting the rate of fire was the availability of ammunition. Through most of its service use, the M109 was accompanied into the field by the M548 cargo carrier, an unarmored tracked vehicle based on the chassis of the M113 armored personnel carrier. However, the ammunition in the M548 was unprotected, and the crew had to laboriously move, unpack, and fuze the ammunition while exposed to enemy fire. During HELBAT 7 in 1979 the Army experimented with an M109 chassis modified with a fixed superstructure on the rear of the hull in place of the turret, which allowed a rapid reloading of the M109 from under armored cover. The concept was so successful that in 1980, a crash program was initiated to deploy the M992 FAASV (Field Artillery Ammunition Support vehicle). Five prototypes were ordered in 1981, the FAASV was type-classified in the spring of 1983, and the initial production series was funded in the 1983 defense budget. The one change from the prototypes to the production vehicle was the deletion of the 1,500lb extensible boom crane fitted on the front of the prototypes. The FAASV was a very simple adaptation of the M109 chassis, with a fixed structure on the rear of the chassis containing honeycomb stowage racks for 93 155mm projectiles, 99 propelling charges and 104 fuzes. During artillery firing operations, the FAASV backed up against the M109, with the rear doors sheltering the crew underneath. Ammunition was passed from the FAASV to the M109 by means of a conveyor tray that

An important innovation in artillery tactics in the 1980s was the adoption of the M992 FAASV artillery supply vehicle based on the M109 chassis. This example is from Battery B, 4-82d Artillery of the 3d Armored Division, seen during a Reforger exercise in the 1980s. The tactical number on the side in a blue rectangle indicates it was part of the "Blue" forces during the wargame. (Pierre Touzin)

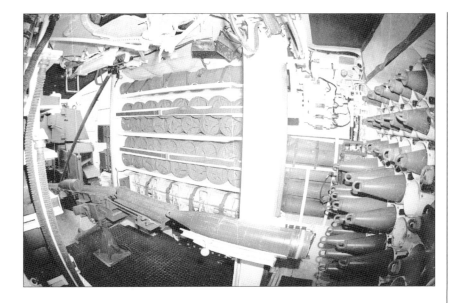

connected between the two vehicles. In total, 664 M992s were built, and the first vehicles were delivered in July 1984. The FAASV first saw combat use during Operation *Desert Storm* in 1991. A derivative of the FAASV for use with the M110A2 8in SPH was developed for trials as the XM1050, but it did not enter serial production.

In the mid-1990s a further 125 M992A1 FAASVs were built, which employed the new 440hp engine from the M109A6 Paladin, had modifi-

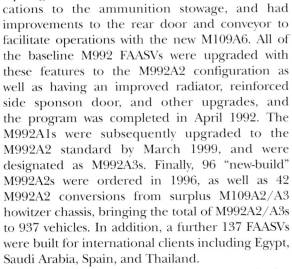

cations to the ammunition stowage, and had improvements to the rear door and conveyor to facilitate operations with the new M109A6. All of the baseline M992 FAASVs were upgraded with these features to the M992A2 configuration as well as having an improved radiator, reinforced side sponson door, and other upgrades, and the program was completed in April 1992. The M992A1s were subsequently upgraded to the M992A2 standard by March 1999, and were designated as M992A3s. Finally, 96 "new-build" M992A2s were ordered in 1996, as well as 42 M992A2 conversions from surplus M109A2/A3 howitzer chassis, bringing the total of M992A2/A3s to 937 vehicles. In addition, a further 137 FAASVs were built for international clients including Egypt, Saudi Arabia, Spain, and Thailand.

The FAASV configuration suggested the possibility of other support variations based on the M109 chassis. A Fire Direction Center Vehicle (FDCV) was built for HELBAT 8. Although there was no series production of the FDCV for the US Army, three vehicles were manufactured by BMY as the Field Artillery Operation Center Vehicle for use at the National Training Center during the Task Force-XXI exercises. While the US Army

The US Army originally planned to deploy the MIM-115 Roland air defense missile system on a version of the M109 chassis, the XM975. Although several were built, the Army subsequently decided to mount the system on a 5-ton truck instead. (US Army)

never bought the FDCV, 119 were sold to foreign customers including 72 to Egypt, 41 to Greece, and six to Taiwan. Other proposed uses included as a mobile evacuation/ambulance vehicle, forward observer vehicle, and different types of armored supply vehicles.

The M109 chassis was also selected to serve as the basis for a launch vehicle for the US Army's MIM-115 air defense missile system, as the XM975. The MIM-115 was a license-produced version of the European Roland missile system adopted by the US Army in 1974. However, the program ran into considerable technical difficulty, and the launch system was eventually switched to a modified M812A1 5-ton truck instead of the XM975. Only one battalion was ever deployed, and the unlucky system was retired after barely a decade in service. Even though the M109 chassis did not serve in the US Army as an air defense vehicle in its intended role, several chassis were converted into mock Soviet air defense systems and are used for training purposes at various US facilities. The first of these was the XM-42S built by the Harry Diamond Labs on surplus M108 chassis to simulate the Soviet ZSU-23-4 Shilka air defense gun. A far more secret conversion was the XM-11S by the Fort Worth Division of General Dynamics which was used to simulate the Soviet Buk (SA-11 Gadfly). Although these vehicles were not precise visual matches for the actual Soviet equipment, they were designed primarily to mimic their radar signature for various types of electronic warfare exercises and testing.

GULF WARS

Operation *Desert Storm*

The war against Iraq in February 1991 saw the most extensive use of the M109 in combat. The M109A6 Paladin was only beginning to enter production, so the M109A2/A3 was still standard. The US Army deployed the equivalent of 25 M109 battalions in the Gulf War, including 15 battalions

One of the most secret versions of the M109 was the XM-11S radar vehicle, built by General Dynamics to simulate the Soviet 9K (SA-11 Gadfly) air defense missile system for various testing and training operations. (General Dynamics)

in the armored and infantry divisions, seven battalions with field artillery brigades, and the equivalent of three battalions with the armored cavalry regiments. These were all regular army battalions except for the 1-201st Field Artillery, a National Guard Battalion. These battalions were under the new "Div-86" organization, with 24 M109A2/A3s in each battalion (apart from three battalions under the pre-1986 organization with only 18 M109 SPHs each). These units amounted to about half of the Army artillery force in the Gulf, the other units being equipped with towed 105mm light guns, the M110 203mm SPH, and the MLRS multiple-launch rocket system. In total, the M109 battalions fired about 43,000 rounds during the fighting. The performance of the M109A2/A3 was satisfactory, though in some of the fast-moving armor units, there was some concern that older vehicles such as the M109 and the M113 armored personnel carriers could not keep pace with the newer generation of vehicles such as the M1A1 Abrams tank and Bradley fighting vehicle. In addition, the M109 could be outranged by Iraqi 155mm guns, but Iraqi artillery was so effectively suppressed that it never posed a significant counter-battery threat.

Desert Storm saw many innovations in the Army artillery. Although the PADS (Position Azimuth Determining System) had been introduced in the 1970s and superseded the laborious manual survey involved in accurately deploying howitzers, in the trackless wastes of the Kuwaiti frontier, such a system was not as useful as in Europe. Units were instead issued with new GPS satellite navigation receivers that allowed the battalions to move across hundreds of miles of featureless desert, and still halt and fire with unprecedented speed and precision. Iraqi counter-battery fire proved less of a threat than feared, as when they fired, they were quickly located by the new Firefinder radars and pummeled by MLRS counter-battery fire. During the initial phases of the war the M109 was forced to rely on the extended-range M549 RAP and maximum charges round because of the distances involved. Once in close-combat range after the offensive started, the DPICM rounds became the preferred choice. The lethality of the M109 was substantially increased by the use of new ammunition, particularly the DPICM rounds. It was discovered after the war that US peacetime estimates of the lethality of the DPICM were significantly understated and that the munition was much more effective in actual use. In addition, the psychological effect was greater than anticipated, and after a horrifying dose of "steel rain," many Iraqi units became ineffective, as their troops desperately scattered to find any cover possible. The M712 Copperhead laser-guided round was something of a disappointment, and only about 100 rounds were fired, although they proved valuable in the artillery raids that preceded the offensive. OH-58D scout helicopters would seek out key Iraqi guards' posts and radar positions, illuminate them with a laser designator, and a single Copperhead round would then be launched. But once the offensive began, it proved too slow and cumbersome to use the Copperhead in most situations, and it was difficult to use when there was fog or cloud cover because the laser beam became attenuated. Operation *Desert Storm* also saw the combat debut of the M992 FAASV artillery resupply vehicle.

The US Marine Corps did not use the M109 as extensively as the Army in the Gulf War. Prior to Operation *Desert Storm*, the Marines Corps was phasing out its M109A3 self-propelled howitzers in favor of the towed M198 155mm howitzer. As a result, of the 11 Marine artillery battalions that served in the war, most relied on the M198. Due to the reliance of some Marine units on materiel pre-positioned in the Gulf on ships, four Marine batteries ended up with M109A3 SPHs: Battery Q, 5-10th Marines; S/5-11th Marines, K and M/4-14th Marines. For example, the 5th Battalion 11th Marine Regiment, the general support artillery battalion of the 1st Marine Division, had two batteries of M198s, one battery of M109A3s, and one battery of M110A1s.

British artillery in the Gulf relied on the M109 as the new AS-90 Braveheart was not yet ready for deployment. The three battalions serving

The most extensive combat use of the M109A2/A3 was during Operation *Desert Storm*. This is an M109A2/A3 of the 41st Artillery, 24th Infantry Division (Mechanized), at Ft Stewart, Georgia, in the spring of 1991 shortly after the unit had returned from the Gulf. The vehicle to the right is an M981 FIST-V forward observer vehicle, a key element in field artillery modernization during the 1980s. (Author)

One of the more unusual vehicles built on the M109 chassis was the Egyptian SP122, which used Egyptian-manufactured copies of the Soviet D-30 howitzer instead of the usual 155mm howitzer. (Christopher Foss)

with the 1st Armoured Division (2, 26, 40 Field Regts., Royal Artillery) all operated the M109, with a total of 60 in the division. The M109 was also used in combat by several of the Allied Arab armies, although it is not at all clear how much combat they actually saw. The Egyptian 4th Armored Division and 3d Mechanized Division belonging to II Corps with Joint Forces Command-North employed the M109A2 in their artillery regiments. Saudi army units also were equipped with the M109A1B and M109A2.

Operation *Iraqi Freedom*

By the time of the 2003 war with Iraq, the M109A6 Paladin was in service with the "Marne Thunder," the divisional artillery of the 3d Infantry Division (Mechanized) that bore the brunt of the US Army fighting on the road to Baghdad. The divisional artillery commander, Col. Thomas Torrance, later summarized his views of the performance of the new equipment in *Field Artillery Journal*: "The combat performance of the M109A6 Paladin was magnificent. It is an extremely capable system that consistently put rounds down-range in less than two minutes after mission receipt, even while on the march. Firing batteries regularly fired from superhighways, narrow secondary roads, and open desert to deliver their munitions with devastating accuracy. The system held up well to the rigors of the battle as shown by our fighting strengths never dropping below 51 of 54 systems."

Operation *Iraqi Freedom* saw many other firsts for the "Redlegs" (the US Artillery), including the first use of the new M7 Bradley FIST (Fire Support Team), and the debut of the AFATDS (Advanced Field Artillery Tactical Data System). Two new projectiles were used for the first time in Iraq by the M109: 108 rounds of the new SADARM precision-guided munition were used for the first time in combat, destroying 48 vehicles. The extended-range M795 high-explosive round also saw its debut, and was much appreciated as it extended the maximum range of the M109 when firing high-explosive from 11 miles (17.5km) to 14 miles (22.5km) compared to the old M107 round. In total, the "Marne Thunder's" M109s fired 13,923 155mm rounds during OIF (Operation *Iraqi Freedom*) in support of the division's infantry and tank battalions. Compared to Operation *Desert Storm* a decade earlier, US Marine artillery had completed the transition to towed M198 155mm guns, and British artillery had replaced their M109s with the new AS-90 Braveheart. Strangely enough, the Iraqis had a small number of M109s on hand, captured from the Iranians in the 1980–88 war, and from Kuwait in 1990.

INTERNATIONAL PROGRAMS

With more than 5,000 M109s and its derivatives exported since 1963, it is not surprising that there have been quite a few local initiatives to modernize the M109. Some of these upgrades have been done using kits provided by US manufacturers, while other countries have developed their own upgrade packages. As a result, very few baseline M109s remain, most having been upgraded at least to M109A1 configuration. Even these are dwindling in number as more vehicles are modernized to M109A3 standards or beyond.

Austria

When Austria acquired 54 new M109A5s in 1997–98, they were configured as the M109A5Oe with several modifications, including an Austrian semi-automatic flick rammer, an inertial navigation system, and a Swiss electrical system.

Belgium

When Belgium decided to retire older M108 and M109 vehicles in 1985 after ordering the M109A2, the Arsenal du Matériel Mécanique et de l'Armement in Rocourt converted 45 of the better chassis into the VBCL (*Véhicule blindé de commandement et de liaison*). These resemble the US Army FAASV in general shape, but are used as a fire direction center vehicle. Each M109 battalion has ten, and they entered service in 1994. Curiously enough, the Belgian Army also decided to re-use the M108 turrets, mating 19 to M109A2 hulls to produce the M108A2B! The rationale for this training vehicle was that there were ample stocks of 105mm ammunition so the vehicle was more economical to operate than the new M109A2.

Egypt

Although Egypt operates some standard M109s, it also ordered a special derivative from BMY in the 1980s called the SP122. This vehicle is based on the M109 chassis, but is armed with a locally manufactured copy of the Soviet D-30 122mm howitzer. A total of 124 SP122s were delivered to Egypt from 1995 to 2000.

Germany

The German Bundeswehr is the largest European NATO operator, and has also been the most active in local M109 upgrades. The original German M109s were modified almost from the start with a new breech to permit the use of more powerful propellant charges, and they were designated as the M109G. In 1983 the Bundeswehr began a further upgrade called M109A3G, which used elements of the US M109A3 upgrade such as the rear bustle rack, but which substituted the Rheinmetall 39-cal. 155mm cannon from the FH-70 towed gun instead of the US cannon. These can be easily distinguished from the US M109A3 conversion by the different muzzle brake, as well as many other local features such as smoke mortars, and drivers' mirrors. Norway's M109A3 fleet was configured on the German pattern as the M109A3GN.

In the late 1990s the German fleet underwent the Rheinmetall Aurora upgrade (*Autonome Richt- und Orientierungsausstattung Rohrartillerie*), and was then designated as M109A3GEA1. This introduced inertial navigation and the IFAB (*Integrierte Feuerleitmittel Artillerie Batterie*) digital communications upgrades. Although the new Panzerhaubitze 2000 began arriving in German artillery battalions in the late 1990s, 262 M109A3Gs were upgraded in 1999–2000 with the Rheinmetall Ammunition Handling

Germany's M109A3G introduced a lengthened 155mm cannon which can be easily distinguished from its American counterpart by the different muzzle brake. Many other German improvements are evident, such as the driver's mirrors, new track, and smoke mortar dischargers. (Rheinmetall)

among the innovations
developed for the Israeli
109L Doher was the Urdan
trail armored ammunition
ailer, a means of re-supplying
e vehicle without the need
r a separate vehicle such as
e FAASV. (Urdan)

Kit (AHK). More might be upgraded depending on the final size of the Bundeswehr artillery force after the cutbacks instituted in 2003.

Israel

Israel introduced a number of minor improvements to its M109 force in the 1980s, most noticeably the addition of large stowage bins on the turret front. Israel was a participant in the US M109 HIP program, and has plans to incorporate some features of this program into its own M109 force as funding permits. The first set of upgrades carried out by the Israeli Ordnance Corps facility at Tel-a-Shomer was codenamed "Doher" and included upgrades to the fire control system, a navigation system upgrade, and NBC protection features. Instead of acquiring a separate ammunition supply vehicle such as FAASV for their artillery battalions, Urdan developed the Artrail which carries a further 44 rounds of ammunition.

Italy

When Italy acquired its first 221 M109s, they were purchased without armament, which was manufactured by OTO Melara based on the modified 155mm howitzer used in the German M109G. Italy decided to follow the German pattern, and in 1986 began modernizing its M109 with the 39-cal. cannon derived from the FH-70 towed 155mm gun. A total of 280 were converted to M109L standards in 1986–92.

Korea (ROK)

The M109A2 was co-produced in the Republic of Korea by Samsung Techwin Defense Products Division up to the early 1990s with 1,040 being completed. This makes South Korea the largest user of the M109 outside the United States.

e Italian M109L upgraded the
seline M109 to M109A1
andard, but used the cannon
om the FH-70 towed gun. This
109L belongs to the 132d
mored Artillery Regiment of
e Ariete Division. (OTO-Melara)

Netherlands

The Dutch firm RDM developed an upgrade kit for the M109 in conjunction with Bofors in Sweden, which includes a new 47-cal. gun, resulting in the M109L47. When the Netherlands Army downsized in the mid-1990s, it disposed of some of its recently upgraded M109A3s, and 85 were sold to the United Arab Emirates after being upgraded with the RDM weapon. In 2001 these vehicles were further upgraded with a new land navigation kit and a fire control update developed by Denel in South Africa. RDM has subsequently developed an additional gun upgrade called Extended Range Ordnance (ERO) with a BAE Systems 52-cal. cannon.

Switzerland

The Swiss army has a substantial inventory of M109s, locally known as the Pz.Haubitze 66 (M109), Pz.Hb. 66/77 (M109A1 upgrades); Pz.Hb. 77 (M109A1B); and Pz.Hb. 88 (new 1988 M109A1B purchase). In 1994 the government-owned Swiss Ordnance Enterprise developed a substantially modernized vehicle with a new 47-cal. cannon derived from the Bison fortress gun. This upgrade also included fire control/navigation upgrades and was called the M109 KAWEST and later Pz.Haubitze 88/95. A total of 348 of these were modernized starting in 1998.

Taiwan

Having purchased M108s in the late 1960s, Taiwan decided to upgrade them in the early 1980s with new weapons. They removed the turret and fitted a 45-cal. 155mm gun on the T-68 and a 155mm howitzer on the T-69.

When the Netherlands Army decided to shed many of its M109 SPHs after the end of the Cold War, RDM developed an upgrade package with a new lengthened gun to make it more attractive to export clients. This M109L47 was one of 85 sold to Abu Dhabi in the United Arab Emirates. (Author)

The Swiss Army modernized its M109 fleet into the Panzer-haubitze 88/95 configuration at the Thun arsenal starting in 1995. The new 155mm gun is derived from the 155mm Bison fortification gun, and many other improvements have been made including a rear turret bustle extension. (Swiss Ordnance)

INTERNATIONAL M109 EXPORTS 1963–2003

Country	M108	M109	M109A1B	M109A2	M109A5	M992 FAASV	FDCV
Austria		38		18	54		
Belgium	18			127			
Brazil	72						
Canada		50*		26			
Denmark		76*					
Egypt				164		51	72
Ethiopia		12					
Germany		609*					
Greece			51	84	24		41
Iran		50*	390				
Israel		60*	369				
Italy		221*	62				
Jordan		126*		108			
Korea (ROK)				1,040			
Kuwait			6	31			
Morocco			36	3			
Netherlands		135*	3	91			
Norway		127*					
Pakistan				152			
Peru			12				
Portugal				14			
Saudi Arabia			87	24		60	
Spain	48	18*	60	6		6	
Switzerland			435				
Taiwan	117			197	28		6
Thailand					20	20	
Turkey	26						
UK			40	69			
Total	**281**	**1,522**	**1,551**	**2,154**	**126**	**137**	**119**

*Later upgraded to M109A1 or -A3 standards

BIBLIOGRAPHY

There are no published books on the M109, though it is covered in many survey accounts of modern US armored vehicles, notably in Richard Hunnicutt's excellent *Sheridan: A History of the American Light Tank* (Presidio, 1995). This book is based in part on a semi-official history entitled *M109 Series SPH* released by the Medium Artillery Division of the US Army Armament, Munitions and Chemical Command, Rock Island in 1985. The best source of coverage of the international aspects of the M109 program can be found in the annual editions of *Jane's Armour and Artillery* by Christopher Foss; the 2001–2002 edition (Jane's Information Group, 2001) was used when preparing this book. Many publications aimed at the defense industry have published a great deal of useful information over the years, and the most valuable in the preparation of this book were *Jane's Defense Weekly, International Defence Review* (both Jane's Information Group), and the Association of the US Army (AUSA) journal, *Army*. On operational aspects of the M109, *Field Artillery Journal* (United States Field Artillery Association) was most useful, particularly on lessons learned during Operation *Desert Storm* and Operation *Iraqi Freedom*. Technical manuals on different variants of the M109 were also informative, and these can be found at some US Army libraries such as the Military History Institute at

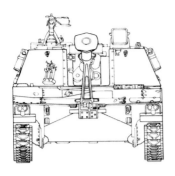 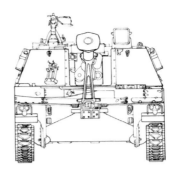

the US Army War College at Carlisle Barracks in Pennsylvania. There are numerous other sources of information on the M109, although these are not usually available to those outside the defense business. For example, many firms such as BMY (now United Defense) released informative brochures on their work on the M109 at annual defense conventions and exhibits, notably the AUSA convention in Washington, DC, the biennial Eurosatory exhibition in Paris, and the biennial IDEX exhibition in the United Arab Emirates. Having covered the armored vehicle business back in the 1970s and early 1980s for DMS Inc., I was able to rely on a large collection of these when preparing this book. For modelers interested in photo coverage of the M109, there is my older book *US Mechanized Firepower Today* (Arms & Armour Press: Tanks Illustrated No. 26, 1987) and Francois Verlinden's *War Machines No. 1: M108-M109-M109A1/A2* (Verlinden, 1990).

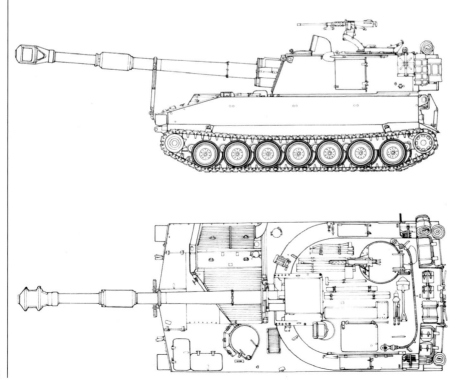

109 155MM SPH, BATTERY A, 1-14TH FIELD ILLERY, 2D ARMORED DIVISION, FT HOOD, AS, 1976

over a half-century of plain Olive Drab finishes, in the 1970s the US Army began to camouflage-paint its oat vehicles. In 1972 the US Mobility Equipment arch and Development Center (MERDC) at Ft Belvoir n experimenting with a variety of camouflage patterns oaints, finally settling on a four-color system in 1973. The rns were designed to be suitable for eight environments: oe/US winter verdant; snow temperate forested; snow erate open terrain; Europe/US summer verdant; verdant cs; gray desert; red desert; arctic winter. The system designed to minimize the need for repainting. So, for nple, vehicles painted in the winter verdant scheme as here, could be switched to the summer verdant scheme ly by re-painting the Field Drab portions with Light n. The patterns relied on 12 camouflage colors which essentially the same as those used by the US Army neers since World War II. The two principal colors red about 45 percent each of the surface, while the two idiary colors covered only about five percent each and mainly intended to break up the pattern. The pattern's distinctive designs were the black "crows' feet" pattern. e same time, the US Army switched from Olive Drab orest Green as its standard tactical camouflage color, all new equipment purchased was delivered from the ufacturer in this color.

he first unit finished in these colors was a brigade of the rmored Division at Ft Hood in the summer of 1973 as here. The winter verdant scheme was actually one e most popular schemes in the southwestern US, as ield Drab color tended to blend with the dried prairie s. The scheme consisted of FS 34079 Forest Green and 0118 Field Drab as the predominant colors, with FS 7 Sand and FS 37038 Black as the subsidiary colors.

The Israeli Ordnance Corps made a number of stowage changes to the M109A1B self-propelled howitzers prior to their debut in combat in the 1982 Lebanon war, notably the large stowage bins on the turret front. (IGPO)

The adoption of the MERDC camouflage patterns was also accompanied by the use of subdued tactical markings. All tactical markings, including registration numbers and bumper codes, were applied in flat black. So here, the symbol of the 14th Field Artillery, the azimuth symbol (Maltese cross) within a circle, is painted in black on the turret front. The bumper codes for this vehicle were: (left) 2Δ1F14 (right) A-26. They were painted on either side of the upper edge of the front bow plate and on either rear fender. This practice was soon found to be impractical since the codes could not be easily read, and in later years, it became the standard practice to paint the bumper codes on a small rectangle of a contrasting color, usually black numbers on a sand rectangle.

The Republic of China in Taiwan modernized its old M108 self-propelled howitzers into the T-68 155mm SPG in the 1980s by removing the turret and mounting a much larger, locally designed 155mm gun. A similar conversion, using a short 155mm howitzer, was built as the T-69. A T-68 is seen here on parade in Taipei in the 1980s. (Just Probst)

An M992 FAASV of Battery A, 1-78th Artillery, at the Field Artillery Training Center at Ft Sill, Oklahoma, painted in the standard NATO three-color scheme. (Author)

B: M109G, NORTHERN BRIGADE, NORWEGIAN ARMY, EXERCISE ARROWHEAD EXPRESS, NORWEGIAN ARCTIC 1988

The Norwegian Army finished its vehicles in a dark forest green color. During some winter exercises, this attractive splinter camouflage of black and white was applied over the dark green color. Norwegian tactical arm-of-service markings were patterned after the British system as seen here. The red "X" markings were a typical NATO improvisation during exercises to mark the "Opposing Forces".

C1: M109A1, DIVARTY, 3D INFANTRY DIVISION, REFORGER EXERCISE, WEINREID, GERMANY, 1977

While the US Army in CONUS (Continental US) was being repainted with the new MERDC camouflage pattern, the US Seventh Army in Germany began to adopt its own expedient camouflage in the early 1970s. The two predominant colors were FS 30277 Sand and FS 30117 Earth Red with smaller areas of FS 34079 Forest Green and FS 37038 Black. The brown color varied more than the others and was sometimes mixed by the troops in depot, leading to erratic results. By the 1980s the MERDC patterns and paint became available, and the Seventh Army began to switch to the standard US Army camouflage, generally the summer verdant scheme. This was short-lived, as in the mid-1980s, NATO decided to standardize a single camouflage system for tactical vehicles patterned on the German scheme, which replaced the MERDC scheme in 1987. This particular vehicle is marked with one of the older wargame markings, a green triangle within a circle to represent the opposing "Trigon" forces. This was a paper symbol, temporarily taped to the vehicle, rather than painted.

C2: M109A3B, 1 ROYAL CANADIAN HORSE ARTILLERY, CANADIAN ARMY, GERMANY, 1986

Canada first acquired the M109 in 1967, and by the 1980s all vehicles had been modernized to the M109A3 standards. Most were deployed with the 4 Canadian Mechanized Brigade Group in Germany. The 1 RCHA began camouflage painting its M109A3B SPHs in 1985 in a band pattern of black, olive drab, and deep green. Markings were the typical subdued black style so common in NATO at the time, including the tactical number on the hull side and the national

maple leaf insignia on the turret side, sometimes in mixed green and black as seen here to blend into the camouflage

D: M109A2, FIELD ARTILLERY TRAINING CENTER, FT SILL, OKLAHOMA, 1995

See plate for full details.

E: M109A3G, 3./PANZERARTILLERIEBATAILLON 25, BRAUNSCHWEIG, GERMANY, 1991

In 1984–85, the German Bundeswehr began to adopt a new three-color camouflage system that was later taken up throughout most of NATO. It was initially painted in the factory on the new Leopard II tank, but subsequently old equipment was repainted, including the M109A3G as seen here. The colors are *Bronzegrün* RAL 6031, *Teerschwarz* RAL 9021 and *Lederbraun* RAL 8027. The bronze green is, in fact, a fairly dull dark green which tends to fade to a slight grayish shade, and the brown typically fades toward the color of dry cocoa powder. The colors are applied in a standard pattern that was developed for each individual vehicle type.

By the mid-1980s, the Bundeswehr had also adopted a set of subdued markings, sometimes called II.Generation to distinguish it from the more colorful markings used previously. The tactical insignia such as the unit insignia based around standard NATO map symbols is painted in a medium gray color that proved to be more readable than the US black markings. Sometimes full-color unit insignia are permitted if they are small enough, so the battalion insignia on this vehicle is painted in gray on the turret, but it repeated in full color under the map symbol in a much smaller size. The German Maltese cross national insignia remains in the standard white and black.

F1: M109A3, 40 FIELD REGIMENT RA, 7TH ARMOURED BRIGADE, 1ST ARMOURED DIVISION, OPERATION *GRANBY*, IRAQ, 1991

British combat vehicles shipped to Kuwait prior to the 1991 war with Iraq were finished in chemical-resistant sand paint. This color is slightly more vivid and mustard than the comparable US Army color. When first deployed in Kuwait, the markings tended to be very simple, the tactical marking in black on the turret door, and the usual style of registration number central on the bow and stern in white numerals on a black rectangle as shown on the inset drawing. Prior to the start of the conflict, most British tactical vehicles had the Coalition's upward-pointing chevron hastily added in black paint. This was usually seen on the hull side of the M109, and the turrets tended to be covered in stowage and kit.

F2: M109A2, BATTERY B, 1-82 FIELD ARTILLERY, 1ST CAVALRY DIVISION, OPERATION *DESERT STORM*, IRAQ 1991

In 1983 the US Army agreed to adopt the new NATO three-color camouflage scheme based on the German system. At the same time, the US Army MERADCOM (Military Equipment Research and Development Command; formerly MERDC) was developing a new paint formulation called CARC (Chemical Agent Resistant Coating), which was a polyurethane paint that did not dissolve like previous enamels and lacquers when washed with chemical decontamination solutions. As a result, when the US Army went over to the new camouflage patterns in 1985, they also adopted the new CARC paint. Besides the three NATO colors, paint was also developed for other environments, notably the desert. So when US forces

...ployed to Kuwait in 1990, CARC Tan 686 was applied to ...ctical vehicles, which is equivalent to FS 33446 Tan.

US tactical vehicles generally had the Coalition's upward-...inting chevron insignia painted on in late January 1991. To ...nfuse matters, US units in Kuwait often used the "spinning ... insignia which had been borrowed from the Israelis, and ...ich resembles the chevron. The direction that the "V" points ...dicates the sub-unit: chevron left, 1st platoon; chevron up, ... platoon; chevron right, 3d platoon. This was usually painted ...ound a tactical number assigned to the various battalions in ...e division. The standard unit bumper codes were painted on ...e front and rear in the usual fashion, and they are shown on ...e accompanying inset drawing.

M109A6 PALADIN, BATTERY B, 1-10TH FIELD ...RTILLERY, 3D BRIGADE, 3D INFANTRY ... VISION (MECHANIZED), OPERATION *IRAQI* ...REEDOM, MARCH 2003

...ring Operation *Iraqi Freedom* in March 2003, US tactical ...hicles were finished in CARC Tan 686, the same as during ...peration *Desert Storm*. Units that arrived later, such as the ...t Armored Division, still had their Paladins in the European ...ATO scheme. The "spinning V" insignia remains in use. The ...ctical numbering seen below the V is based on a system ...opted in 1989 which assigns a double-digit number to each ... the division's ten maneuver battalions (00, 10, 20, 30, 90) ...th the second numeral identifying the sub-unit within the bat-...ion. So 30 identifies the headquarters/headquarters battery ...HB), 31 Alpha Battery, 32 Bravo Battery, 33 Charlie Battery, ...d so on. The individual gun was sometimes identified on the ...ret rear with a large number, in this case a roman numeral I. ...e rectangular panel that resembles a set of Venetian blinds ... the rear center of the turret between the tactical markings is ...Combat Identification Panel (CIP). This panel was developed ...er Operation *Desert Storm* as a means to reduce friendly fire ...idents. Fratricide incidents were most common at night ...en the tactical markings on the vehicle were not evident. ...e CIP is made from material that stands out from the rest of

ABOVE **The M109A1 can be distinguished from the later M109A2 and -A3 by the lack of a ballistic cover over the gunner's sight and the lack of a rear ammunition bustle extension. "Armageddon" is a vehicle of the British Royal Artillery Regiment, which operated 40 M109A1 SPHs. (Simon Dunstan)**

the vehicle when viewed through the thermal imaging night vision systems and is usually carried on the front of the vehicle, though the front panels are not evident in this view.

BELOW **Further upgrades have been developed for the M109, including this Dutch proposal to mount a 52-cal. ERO cannon. It is seen here on display at the 2002 Eurosatory arms show. (Author)**

INDEX

Figures in **bold** refer to illustrations